The Litt
Manet

Catherine de Duve

Discover the life and work of the Father of modernity

KATE'ART
EDITIONS

Paris lit up!
Paris enlarged,
Paris sanitised!

At the order of Emperor Napoleon III and Prefect Haussmann, Paris is becoming a modern city. Streets are being widened and lengthened, buildings erected, squares created and parks set up to make the city beautiful.

In his studio, the young Edouard Manet doesn't paint like his contemporaries. He wants to paint what he sees, modern day life: paved streets, hackney cabs, shop signs. He invents modernity…

 Finish drawing this modern city painted by Manet.

MANET'S TIME

Meanwhile, in the Tuileries Gardens, the upper classes in top hats, monocles, crinolines (large, extravagant dresses) and parasols relax under the shade of the trees.

This painting was exhibited in 1863, the year Napoleon III opened new exhibition spaces to show artworks that had been refused by the jury of the official Salon. It's the new "Salon of Rejects".

 Look for the children having fun making sand castles. What are they wearing?

Edouard

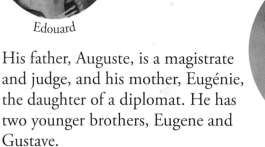

Edouard Manet was born into the ranks of the *bourgeoisie* (wealthy, middle class) on 23rd January 1832, in Paris.

His father, Auguste, is a magistrate and judge, and his mother, Eugénie, the daughter of a diplomat. He has two younger brothers, Eugene and Gustave.

His father and mother

As a child, Edouard takes drawing lessons. He wants to become a painter. But his parents have other plans for their first-born. He's to attend the Naval Academy! He twice fails the examination to join the Navy and so embarks on a training vessel. He sails to Brazil and draws caricatures of the crew during the crossing.

Rubens

Boucher

At long last Manet can pursue an art education. He meets the painter Delacroix who spurs him on. He copies the old masters in the Louvre Museum.

For six years, Edouard takes painting classes in a famous artist's studio, but he'd rather follow his own instinct than his master's advice.

The three Manet brothers take piano lessons with Suzanne Leenhoff, a young Dutch woman, whom Edouard will later marry.

Suzanne

Family secret? Léon Leenhoff is Suzanne's son and Edouard his father apparently. He was conceived out of wedlock and was often introduced as Suzanne's younger brother in order to avoid any form of scandal.

Léon

Berthe

Eugène will later marry Berthe Morisot, Edouard's favourite model and friend. She's also an accomplished painter.

Eugène

Your turn now. Draw your family in the little frames and write down their names.

LOLA

Spain is all the rage! Empress Eugenie is Spanish. A Spanish ballet troupe is touring Paris. Manet paints the dancers in their traditional costumes. He paints a full-length portrait of Lola of Valencia, the star dancer. It's his first masterpiece!

Notice how the black brings out the shimmering colours that Lola's wearing.

Baudelaire writes a quatrain (a poem made up of four lines) which is exhibited alongside the painting: *Lola of Valencia* in 1863.

Among such beauties as one can see everywhere,

I understand, my friends, that desire hesitates;

But one sees sparkling in Lola of Valencia

The unexpected charm of a black and rose jewel.

Manet admires the Spanish masters such as Velázquez (1599-1660) and Goya (1746-1828). He thinks highly of the lack of detail in their work and yet how they achieve this through a very precise way of painting.
He adopts their range of plain tones.
Did Manet draw his inspiration from a portrait by Goya?

Goya, *The Duchess of Alba*, painted in 1797

Compare Goya's painting to Manet's.

Colour in the Spanish dancer's traditional costume.

LUNCHEON ON THE GRASS

On the edge of a wood, in the half-light, two women – one bathing, the other sitting in the nude – casually talk with two fully clothed men. "What indecency!" exclaims Empress Eugénie upon seeing the large canvas. At the time, no one understands this enigmatic painting. Never has such a painting been seen before!

This painting is an invitation for young impressionists such as Claude Monet, to paint in the open air.

The different styles are all mixed together. It looks like a collage. Manet has the gift of giving as much importance to an object as he does to a figure*. Which bit of this painting do you like best?

The Picnic, Monet

Notice every detail and find the different genres: still life, nude, portrait, romantic setting, landscape, abstract foliage.

* *To find out more, read "Long Live Impressionnism and Pointillism!": p. 6-7*

OLYMPIA

In Italy, Edouard Manet discovers the Venetian artist Titian's painting, The Venus of Urbino. He copies it and draws inspiration from it a decade later when he paints Olympia. It sparks considerable controversy when it's exhibited in 1864! The guards must keep disgusted visitors from puncturing and tearing visitors from puncturing or tearing the painting with their walking sticks! But why such an uproar?

Artists have always depicted men and women in the nude. But they're always gods and goddesses. Titian painted Venus, the goddess of love.

Compare Titian's Venus below, with Manet's Olympia opposite.

The Venus of Urbino, Titien, 1538

Manet sought inspiration from classical paintings. So why all the fuss around Olympia? Here he depicts a real woman in the flesh, not a goddess. She is being presented with a bouquet of flowers from a suitor and gazes straight at us. Who is this woman? She's the model Victorine Meurent, not a goddess.

Find the women's small pet.

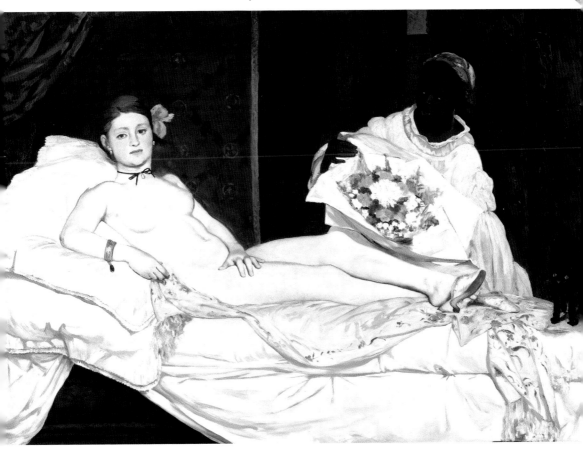

* To find out more, read "Long Live Impressionnism and Pointillism!": p. 4-5

CORRIDA

Manet is fascinated by Spanish culture. He imagines bullfights. The bull charges the bullfighters in the ring. The massive beast gores the picador's horse. The screaming crowd in the stands becomes a dark and blurry mass. Soon it will be the matador's turn to impress the crowd with his passes with the *muleta*, a red cloth that is brandished to excite the bull. The spectators shout *"Olé!"* The bullfight concludes with the killing of the bull by a single sword thrust, known as the *estocada*.

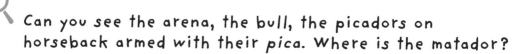

Can you see the arena, the bull, the picadors on horseback armed with their *pica*. Where is the matador?

The matador salutes the spectators in his "suit of lights", a flamboyant gold coloured costume. The crowd praises his agility, grace and bravery. What does he have in his hands?

Imagine the bullfight around the matador. Draw it.

In his studio, Manet remembers a painting he saw in Madrid by Velázquez. The figure dressed in black stands out from a blank background.

Manet now takes up his brush and paints his own version, a young boy in uniform. The colours applied carefully so as to give no relief, form flat patches. The silhouette of the boy stands out from the neutral background. The black forms a neat contour. It only takes him a few loose brushstrokes to emphasise the style of the trousers. The effect is monumental!

Pablo de Valladolid painted by Velázquez c.1635

Colour in the fifer imitating Manet's style. Choose two contrasting colours.

Despite Zola's enthusiasm, the jury of the 1866 Salon turns down the painting. How about you, do you like this painting? What are your impressions when you look at it?

What instrument is he playing? The fife is a small shrill flute made of wood. It is used to give signals to soldiers on the battlefield. Only boys too young to fight take on this role.

THE UNIVERSAL EXHIBITION

The *Exposition Universelle* of 1867 is in full swing and millions of visitors have come to the Champ de Mars in Paris to look at the many pavilions and to ride in the bateaux-mouches, the cruise boats on the river Seine. Kings and queens from all over the world have journeyed to Paris to enjoy the fair. Not far from there, just next to Alma Bridge, Manet exhibits fifty of his paintings in a pavilion he has paid for himself. Look for the hot air balloons and the exhibition pavilions.

Manet is a real city-dweller. He prefers the town to the country. He paints very few landscapes. Here's one. A view of the Trocadero. Long live Paris!

What's that in the sky? A hot air balloon. The empress is heading on up. The view from up there is spectacular!

But 1867 also heralds the end of the Second Mexican Empire. Napeoleon III abandons Emperor Maximilian of Habsburg to his fate when he withdraws his troops. Maximilian will not consider deserting, and is soon taken captive and condemned to death. Here he is looking heroic!

Manet imagines the emperor's execution alongside two of his faithful generals. The soldiers are wearing French uniforms. The sergeant sporting a red hat and loading his weapon, looks just like Napoleon III. How about that?

Is Manet denouncing France's behaviour? Despite its historical depiction, the painting is rejected by the Salon, and even the lithograph is censored!

The emperor Maximilian is wearing a sombrero. Find him.

EMILE ZOLA

Manet is friends with writers and poets such as Baudelaire, Zola, and later on Mallarmé.

"Manet's place is destined to be in the Louvre!", states Zola. Manet's talent goes unnoticed for some years and so Zola publishes a brochure about the artist. To thank him, Manet paints a portrait of him.

Zola strikes a pose in his friend's studio. The decor highlights his taste and calling as a writer. What is he reading?

Look closely at the details in the painting and find the reproduction of Olympia, the engraving according to Velázquez, the Japanese print of the wrestler, the leather bound books, the writer's inkwell and quill, the brochure, the open book by Charles Blanc entitled "*The History of All Painters of All Nations*" and the Japanese screen.

THE BALCONY

In 1868, Manet meets Berthe Morisot, who copics paintings at the Louvre just like him. She becomes his student and model, and will later marry his brother Eugène. Here she is on the balcony!

Who is on the balcony? Manet uses his friends and family as models. The figures are very static, just like in a photograph. What are they doing? Where are they? They're absorbed in their own world and aren't communicating amongst themselves.

Once again the public does not understand this painting. Some mutter "Close the shutters!", when they see it. Manet really does have a surprising way of painting. The green of the rail and shutters is in marked contrast to the white chiffon dresses and the feebly lit backdrop. The colours are harsh and the faces barely detailed. "It looks as if it was badly painted."

Berthe Morisot, painter

Antoine Guillemet, landscape painter

Fanny Claus, violinist

Find each figure. What are they thinking about? Write their thoughts in the bubbles.

Léon Leenhoff, musician

THE BOAT

In the summer of 1873, the Manet family holidays at Berck-sur-Mer, in northern France. Suzanne, engrossed in her book, wears a dress that is loosely painted by the master of the brush stroke. It is Manet's "modern way" of painting. How does she protect herself from the wind and sun? It was fashionable to be pale at the time. Eugène is gazing out to sea. What can he see?

The figures seem to form sandcastles. The sea is a gradation of colour, from dark ultramarine blue to emerald green. The painting has an indefinable melancholic feel to it…

Make up a title for this painting ....

Everything is new about this painting! The abrupt cropping of the boat and sail, the colours… It feels as if we're in the boat with them.

Continue drawing the boat.

MANET & MONET

At Argenteuil

Manet is friends with Degas, Renoir, Pissarro and Monet. Have you heard of them? They are the Impressionists, young artists who are on the fringe of traditional art. However, Manet doesn't want to exhibit his work alongside theirs, even though he's considered their master. He still hopes to be admitted to the Salons and to receive the official honours.

Edouard Manet pays a visit to Claude Monet who, at the time, lived at Argenteuil near Paris, on the banks of the Seine. Auguste Renoir is also there. Both of them paint the Monet family in the garden.

**What are Claude, Camille and Jean doing?
Find the chick, the fan and the watering can.**

24

Claude Monet had a studio-barge built, so he could better observe the strange effects of light on water. What a great idea! Manet depicts Monet painting with Camille for company. The brush strokes are incisive and rapidly executed. A few short 'broken' black brush strokes and a face appears. The paintbrush dances across the canvas, the artist's having fun!

Pay attention to Manet's brush strokes. Find the easel, the oar and the factory chimneys.

MODERN ART

Is Manet the inventor of Modern Art? Besides, what is Modern Art? The artist creates scandals without meaning to. He wants to paint modern day life, and rejects the traditional standards for painting. He paints freely, without any taboos!

What is modern? Topics taken from daily life like this painting.

Moreover, it's a new technique. Having broken free from the rules, Manet paints quickly. His canvases look unfinished. He uses pure colours, considerably influencing the impressionist painters.

In Pere Lathuille's garden, a couple sit at a table chatting. Why does the waiter turn around? The young man is courting a young lady. Manet depicts what he sees around him. That's modernity.

Modernity takes hold of towns, train stations are built. Manet paints the Saint-Lazare train station, which is next to his studio. A child looking through the railings marvels at the smoke and steam billowing up from the locomotive. Manet likes the colour black.

It's your turn now to draw something 'modern' using a "modern" technique.

This is Manet's last great painting. Suzon is a waitress at the bar at the Folies-Bergère nightclub. Manet asks her to pose for him. He imagines her behind the bar lost in thought. The marble counter is full of bottles, flowers and oranges. Behind, a mirror reflects the crowded room and balconies full of customers. Can you see the chandeliers? Who is Suzon speaking to? Us or someone else? Funny feeling…

Compare the poster to the painting. Are there any similarities?

Look at the details and place them back in the painting. Find the trapeze artist.

CAFÉ-CONCERT

Beer

There's a lively atmosphere in the cabaret Reichshoffen! Everyone, the *bourgeoisie*, workmen and artists alike, comes here to relax. Art isn't only created in studios or in the open air, but also in *cafés*. Manet is discussing Art with his artist friends. What are they drinking? Who's smoking a pipe?

Find the dancer, the bass player and the stage curtain.

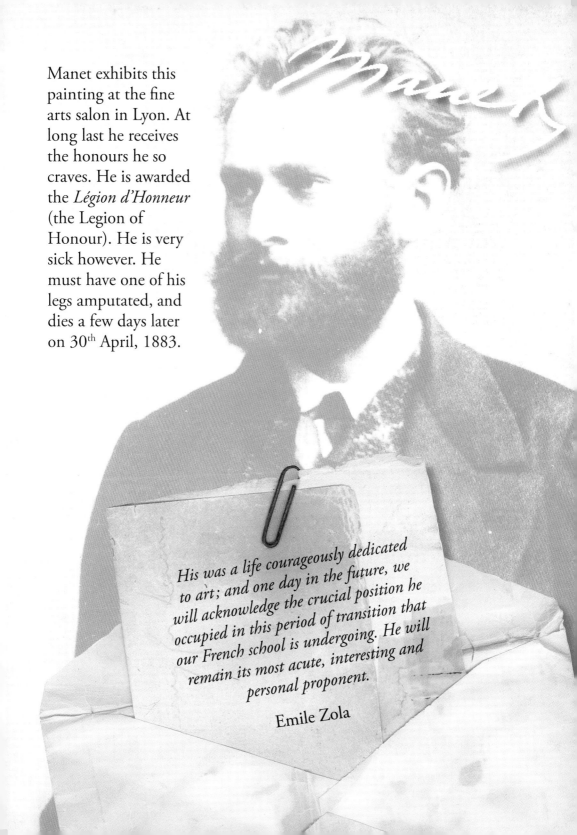

Manet exhibits this painting at the fine arts salon in Lyon. At long last he receives the honours he so craves. He is awarded the *Légion d'Honneur* (the Legion of Honour). He is very sick however. He must have one of his legs amputated, and dies a few days later on 30th April, 1883.

His was a life courageously dedicated to art; and one day in the future, we will acknowledge the crucial position he occupied in this period of transition that our French school is undergoing. He will remain its most acute, interesting and personal proponent.

Emile Zola

Text: Catherine de Duve

Concept and coordination: Kate'Art Editions

Adaptation into English: Kerry-Jane Lowery

PHOTOGRAPHY CREDITS:

Edouard Manet:
Paris: Musée d'Orsay: *The Fifer,* 1866 : cover, p. 1, pp.14-15 - *Portrait of Monsieur and Madame Auguste Manet,* 1860 : p. 4 – *Suzanne at the Piano,* 1867-1868: p. 5 – *Luncheon on the Grass,* 1863 : p. 5, pp.8-9 - *The Balcony,* 1868-1869: p. 5, pp.20-21 - *Lola of Valencia,* 1862 : pp.6-7 - *Olympia,* 1863 : pp.10-11 – *Bullfight,* 1865-1866: p. 12 – *Portrait of Emile Zola, 1867-1868:* pp.18-19 – *At the Beach,* 1873 : p. 22 –
London: National Gallery: *Music in the Tuileries Gardens,* 1862 : p. 3 – *Corner of a Café-Concert,* 1879 : p. 30 – Courtauld Institute: *A Bar at the Folies-Bergère,* 1881 – 1882: pp. 28-29 - **Oslo:** Nationalgalleriet: *The Universal Exhibition of 1867,* 1867: p. 16 – **Tournai:** Museum of Fine Arts: *Argenteuil,* 1874 : p. 24 – *At Père Lathuille's,* 1879 : p. 26 – **Madrid:** Thyssen-Bornemisza Museum: *Amazon,* 1882 : inside cover - **Mannheim:** Städtische Kunsthalle: *The Execution of the Emperor Maximilian,* 1867 : p. 17 – **Munich:** Bayerische Staatsgemäldesammlungen, Neue Pinakothek: *The Luncheon,* 1868 : p. 5 – *Claude Monet Painting On His Studio Boat,* 1874 : p. 25 – **Washington D.C.:** National Gallery of Art: *The Railway,* 1872-1873: p. 27 – **New York:** The Metropolitan Museum of Art: *A Matador (Le Matador Saluant),* 1866-1867: p. 13 – *On a Boat* 1874 : pp. 22-23 – *The Monet Family in Their Garden at Argenteuil,* 1874 : p. 24 - Frick Collection: *The Bullfight,* 1864: p. 13 – **Private Collection:** *La Rue Mosnier aux Paveurs,* 1878 : p. 2 – *Self-Portrait with a Palette,* 1879 : p. 1

Other:
Paris: Musée d'Orsay: Monet, *The Picnic,* 1865-1866: p. 9 – Louvre: Boucher, *Diana Leaving Her Bath,* 1742 : p. 4 – **Madrid:** Museo del Prado: Velázquez, *Pablo de Vallodolid,* c.1635 : p. 14 – **Munich:** Bayerische Staatsgemäldesammlungen, Alte Pinakothek: Rubens: *Helena Fourment with her Son Francis,* 1660-1664: p. 4 – **Florence:** Galleria degli Uffizi: Titian: *Venus of Urbino,* c.1538 : p. 10 – **New York:** The Hispanic Society of America: Francisco de Goya: *Duchess of Alba,* 1797: p. 7

Archives:
Hôtel Helder: p. 2 – *Overview of the Palace of Industry, a cast iron and glass construction, by the engineer Krantz:* p. 16 – *Folies Bergère Poster:* p. 29 – *Photograph of Manet,* c.1865 : p. 31

Thank you to: Stuart Forward, Eric Vaes, Véronique Lux, Kerry Jane Lowery and all the people who helped to make this book.